THE ESSENTIAL HANDBOOK
of
VICTORIAN
ETIQUETTE

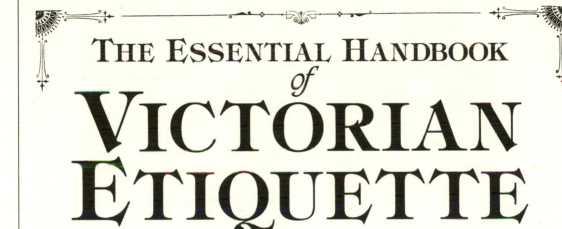

THE ESSENTIAL HANDBOOK
of
VICTORIAN ETIQUETTE

Professor Thomas E. Hill

A Bluewood Book

Critical acclaim accorded Professor Hill's first edition:

"Admirably arranged and handsomely illustrated,
forming the most comprehensive and
satisfactory work of the kind I have ever seen."
—Schyler Colfax,
Vice-President of the United States (1869-1873)

"Let it be placed where young people may have access to
it; and in the hands of every family, where children can,
as it were, grow up with it, so that its principles may be a
kind of second nature to them."
—*Akron Beacon*

"A work of which no written description can give a
properly adequate idea. It must be examined, that its
merits may be appreciated. The author seems to have
studied the wants of almost every person and family, and
more perfectly met these wants than it would seem
possible to do in volumes; and yet we find it in one
compact book, which comes within the reach of all."
—*Easton Free Press*

"One of the most useful volumes that was ever laid upon the drawing room table."
—*Chicago Evening Post*

"I know of no work that contains so great a variety of information on social topics. I think it a work of special value to those who have not had opportunities of an extended school course, or becoming familiar by contact with the conventionalities of society."
—*D.S. Burns, Superintendent of Public Schools*

"I had presented myself at President Grant's cottage, tipped and doffed my hat, announced my business, when the president promptly said he did not want to subscribe. I obtained permission to show it to him, and did so very hurriedly. At the conclusion, he took my specimen copy, paid me in cash, and added his name to my autograph book."
—*An agent for the first edition of*
Professor Hill's Handbook

he absence of good etiquette is more than just bad manners. It can also be fatal. As Professor Hill points out:

"Some evening callers make themselves odious by continuing their visit too long, and even when they have risen to depart they lack decision of purpose to go, but will frequently stand several minutes before taking final leave, and then will stand in the doorway to tell one more story while the hostess protects herself as best she can from the incoming gusts of wind and storm, sometimes taking a cold that ends in death."

Let that be, in the immortal words of Monty Python, a warning to you all!

This edition was produced in 1994 by Bluewood Books and
adapted directly from material written and published by
Professor Thomas E. Hill between 1873 and 1890.
This edition was published in 1994 by Bluewood Books, a division of
The Siyeh Group, Inc., 38 South B Street, San Mateo, CA 94401

ISBN 0-912517-12-3

Printed in USA

Edited by William P. Yenne

Designed by Thomas V. Debolski and Ruth E. DeJauregui

Cover illustration adapted from a series of illustrations by
Charles Dana Gibson, creator of the immortal Gibson Girl.

Interior illustrations by Charles Dana Gibson and from a portfolio of
illustrations commissioned by Professor Hill himself.

Table of Contents

PREFACE

***

n the actual words of the nineteenth century's master of manners, *The Essential Handbook of Victorian Etiquette* is the best of a bygone time when gentlemen were gentlemen, ladies were ladies and they all carefully read these words to know everything from who they should marry to the *proper* way to refuse soup at a formal dinner.

More than a century has passed since Professor Thomas E. Hill published such works as *Morals & Manners Illustrated* and his *Manual of Social and Business Forms.* He categorized the etiquette that governed an entire epoch. He literally defined the lifestyle of a generation, a lifestyle against which the rascals of the Roaring Twenties would ultimately rebel. Professor Hill directed the proper American man and woman on the "approved methods in speaking and acting in the various relations of life." Now he's back in his original words with *The Essential Handbook of Victorian Etiquette.*

Today, propriety has been replaced by "political correctness" and we can look back with nostalgia and amusement upon Professor Hill's era, but in his words there is a grain of civility and polish that we could do well to heed, or at least consider.

So, with that in mind, we may pick up the correct fork and dig into this delicious collection of Victorian society's dos and don'ts, musts and mustn'ts.

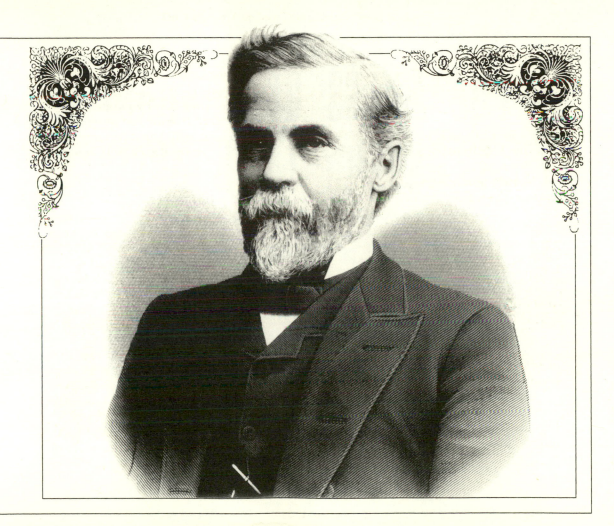

The Rules of Conduct That Govern Good Society

To some, a pleasing manner comes very naturally. If born to the possession of an easy flow of language, agreeableness of address, poetical and imaginative power, and large knowledge of human nature, the whole accompanied by judicious training, good education and wide opportunities, such persons will most surely, without studied effort, be self-possessed and at ease in any company, upon any occasion.

On the contrary, if the natural advantages have been few, and the opportunities for acquiring polished deportment limited, then we may very appropriately make a study of the subject of how to please.

Hence we have the necessity for special instruction on the Subject of Etiquette.

THE ETIQUETTE OF INTRODUCTIONS.

lways apply the titles when making introductions where the persons are entitled to the same, such as Honorable, Reverend, Professor, etc. Thus, in introducing a clergyman to a member of the legislature, it is etiquette to say: "Mr. Shelden, permit me to present to you the Reverend Mr. Wing."

Addressing Mr. Shelden, he says: "Mr. Wing is the pastor of the First Presbyterian Church at Troy, New York."

Addressing Mr. Wing, he continues: "Mr. Shelden is at present our representative in the State Legislature, and author of *The Shelden Letters* which you have so admired."

To approach another in a boisterous manner, saying, "Hello, Old Fellow!," "Hello, Bob" or using kindred expressions, indi-

cates ill-breeding. If approached, however, in this vulgar manner, it is better to give a civil reply, and address the person respectfully, in which case he is quite likely to be ashamed of his own conduct.

Husbands and wives indicate pleasant conjugal relation existing when they address each other in the family circle by their Christian names, though the terms of respect, "Mr." and "Mrs.," may be applied to each among strangers.

GENERAL RULES OF ETIQUETTE.

☞ Never point at another person.

☞ Never wantonly frighten others.

☞ Never make yourself the hero of your own story.

☞ Never pick your teeth or clean your nails in company.

☞ Never question a servant or a child about family matters.

☞ Never read letters which you may find addressed to others.

☞ Never call attention to the features or form of anyone present.

☞ Never seem to notice a scar, deformity, or defect of anyone present.

When speaking to a boy under fifteen years of age, outside of the circle of relatives, among comparative strangers, call him by his Christian name, such as "Charles," "William," etc.

Above that age, if the boy has attained good physical and intellectual development, apply the "Mr." as in "Mr. Brown," "Mr. King," etc. To do so will please him, will raise his self-respect, and will be tendering a courtesy which you highly valued when you were of the same age.

It is an insult to address a boy or girl who is a stranger to you as "Bub" or "Sis." Children are sometimes very sensitive on these points, resenting such method of being addressed, while they very highly appreciate being spoken to respectfully. Thus, if the child's name is unknown, to say "My Boy," or "My Little Lad," "My Girl," or "My Little Lady," will be to gain favor and set the child a good example in politeness. Children forever gratefully remember those who treat them respectfully.

The inferior is to be introduced to the superior; the younger to the older; the gentleman to the lady.

To shake hands when introduced is optional; between gentlemen it is common,

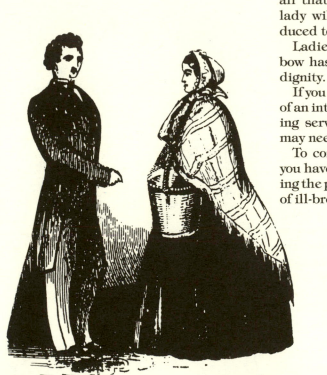

and oftentimes between an elderly and a young person. It is not common between an unmarried lady and a gentleman, a slight bow between them when introduced being all that etiquette requires. The married lady will use her discretion when introduced to gentlemen.

Ladies being introduced should never bow hastily, but with slow and measured dignity.

If you are a gentleman, do not let the lack of an introduction prevent you from rendering services to any unattended lady who may need them.

To completely ignore another to whom you have been rightly introduced, by meeting the person with a vacant stare, is a mark of ill-breeding.

THE ETIQUETTE OF SHAKING HANDS.

Offer the whole hand. It is an insult, and indicates snobbery, to present two fingers *(Fig. 1)* when shaking hands. It is also insulting to return a warm, cordial greeting with a lifeless hand *(Fig. 2)*, an evident indifference of manner, when hand-shaking.

Present a cordial grasp *(Fig. 3)* and clasp the hand firmly, shaking it warmly for a period of two or three seconds, and then relinquishing the grasp entirely. It is rude to grasp the hand very tightly or to shake it over-vigorously. To hold it a very long time is often very embarrassing, and is a breach of etiquette.

In shaking hands, as an evidence of cordiality, regard, and respect, offer the right hand, unless the same be engaged; in which case, apologize, by saying "Excuse my left hand." It is the right hand that carries the sword in time of war, and its extension is emblematic of friendliness in time of peace.

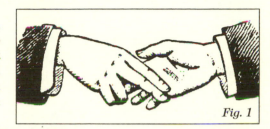

Fig. 1

Fig. 2

Fig. 3

THE ETIQUETTE OF CONVERSATION.

o acquire the art of conversation in a superior degree, there must be intimacy with those who possess refinement and general information. There must also be observed certain general rules in order to accomplish the best results, prominent among which are the following:

☞ Be cool, collected, and self-possessed, using respectful, chaste, and appropriate language.

☞ Recollect that the object of conversation is to entertain and amuse.

☞ Be patient. The foreigner cannot, perhaps, recall the word he desires; the speaker may be slow of speech; you may

have heard the story a dozen times; but even then you must evince interest and listen patiently through.

☞ Do not always commence a conversation by an allusion to the weather.

☞ Do not, when narrating an incident, continually say "you see," "you know," etc.

☞ Do not use profanity, vulgar terms, slang, phrases, words of double meaning, or language that will bring the blush to any person.

☞ Do not intersperse your language with foreign words and high-sounding terms. It shows affectation, and will draw ridicule upon you.

☞ Do not make a pretense of gentility, nor parade the fact that you are a descendant of any notable family. You must pass for just what you are, and must stand on your own merit.

☞ Do not make a parade of being acquainted with distinguished or wealthy people, of having been to college, or of

having visited foreign lands. All this is no evidence of any real genuine worth on your part.

☞ Do not use the surname alone when speaking of your husband or wife to others. To say to another, that "I told Jones," referring to your husband, sounds badly, whereas, to say, "I told Mr. Jones," shows respect and good breeding.

☞ Do not attempt to pry into the private affairs of others by asking what their profits are, what things cost, whether Melissa ever "had a beau," and why Amarette never got married.

☞ Do not aspire to be a great storyteller. An inveterate teller of long stories becomes very tiresome. To tell one or two witty, short, new stories, appropriate to the occasion, is about all that one person should inflict on the company.

☞ Do not indulge in satire; no doubt you are witty, and you could say a most cutting thing that would bring the laugh of the company upon your opponent, but you must not allow it, unless to rebuke an impertinent fellow who can be suppressed in no other way.

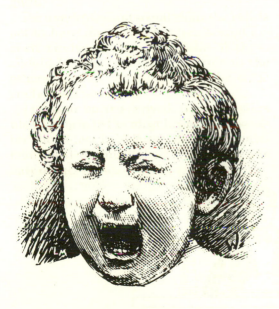

GENERAL RULES OF ETIQUETTE.

☞ Never punish your child for a fault to which you are addicted yourself.

☞ Never, when traveling abroad, be over-boastful in praise of your own country.

☞ Never lend an article you have borrowed unless you have permission to do so.

☞ Never exhibit anger, impatience, or excitement when an accident happens.

☞ Never will a gentleman allude to conquests which he may have made with ladies.

☞ Never fail to offer the easiest and best seat in the room to an invalid, an elderly person, or a lady.

THE ETIQUETTE OF CALLING.

t is customary, according to the code of etiquette, to call all the hours of daylight morning, and after nightfall evening. In making a formal call, a lady does not remove her bonnet or wraps. A gentleman, making a formal call in the morning, must retain his hat in his hand. He may leave his umbrella and cane in the hall, but not his hat and gloves. The fact of retaining his hat indicates a formal call.

When a gentleman accompanies a lady at a morning call (which is seldom), he assists her up the steps, rings the bell, and follows her into the reception-room. It is for the lady to determine when they should leave.

Calls from people living in the country are expected to be longer and less ceremonious than from those in the city.

Among the disagreeable callers are the husband and wife who come with a child and a small dog; the husband making himself familiar with the hostess, the dog barking at the cat, the child taking the free run of the house, while the wife, in the meantime, passes around the room, handling and examining the ornaments. Another unpleasant caller is the man just in out of the rain, whose overcoat and umbrella drips on the carpet.

What Should Be Avoided When Calling.

☞ Do not stare around the room.

☞ Do not take a dog or small child.

☞ Do not lay aside the bonnet at a formal call.

☞ Do not fidget with your cane, hat, or parasol.

☞ Do not make a call of ceremony on a wet day.

☞ Do not touch the piano, unless invited to do so.

☞ Do not handle ornaments or furniture in the room.

☞ Do not make a display of consulting your watch.

☞ Do not go to the room of an invalid, unless invited.

☞ Do not continue the call longer when conversation begins to lag.

☞ Do not remain when you find the lady upon the point of going out.

☞ Do not open or shut doors or windows or alter the arrangement of the room.

A gentleman, though a stranger, may with propriety escort an unattended lady to the carriage, and afterward return to make his farewell bow to the hostess.

Unless invited to do so, it is a violation of etiquette to draw near the fire for the purpose of warming one's self. Should you, while waiting the appearance of the hostess, have done so, you will arise upon her arrival, and then take the seat she may assign you.

When a lady has set apart a certain evening for receiving calls, it is not usual to call at other times, except if the excuse should be business reasons.

All uncouth and ungraceful positions are especially unbecoming among ladies and gentlemen in the parlor. Thus, standing with the arms akimbo, sitting astride a chair, wearing a hat, leaning back in the chair, standing with legs crossed, feet on the chairs, and smoking in the presence of ladies—all those acts evince lack of polished manners.

The practice of issuing personal notes of invitation, which is sometimes done, to a list of gentlemen acquaintances, stating that certain ladies will receive is not to be recommended. It looks very much like begging the gentlemen to come and see them; moreover, should the practice generally prevail, it would, in a brief time, abolish New Year's calls altogether, as gentlemen would not feel at liberty to make calls unless personally invited.

It is customary for the ladies who announce that they will receive to make their parlors attractive on that day, and present themselves in full dress. No intoxicating drinks should be allowed.

The illustration at right depicts some behavior to be avoided when calling: (1) standing with arms akimbo, (2) sitting with elbows on the knees, (3) sitting astride the chair and wearing a hat indoors, (4) standing with a hand on the wall and legs crossed, (5) resting a foot on a chair cushion, (6) tipping back on the chair and smoking in the presence of ladies.

What Should Be Avoided When Calling.

☞ Do not enter a room without first knocking and receiving an invitation to come in.

☞ Do not walk around the room, examining pictures, while waiting for the hostess.

☞ Do not introduce politics, religion, or weighty topics for conversation when making calls.

☞ Do not call upon a person in reduced circumstances with a display of wealth, dress, and equipage.

☞ Do not tattle. Do not carry gossip from one family to another.

☞ Do not, if a gentleman, seat yourself upon the sofa beside the hostess, or in near proximity, unless invited to do so.

☞ Do not, if a lady, call upon a gentleman (except officially or professionally) unless he may be a confirmed invalid.

☞ Do not take a strange gentleman with you, unless positively certain that his introduction will be received with favor.

Some evening callers make themselves odious by continuing their visit too long, and even when they have risen to depart they lack decision of purpose to go, but will frequently stand several minutes before taking final leave, and then will stand in the doorway to tell one more story while the hostess protects herself as best she can from the incoming gusts of wind and storm, sometimes taking a cold that ends in death. When the guest is ready to go—*go*.

THE ETIQUETTE OF VISITING.

Before making a visit, you should be perfectly certain that your visit will be agreeable. It is common for some people to be very cordial, and even profuse in their offers of hospitality. They unquestionably mean what they say at the time, but when they tender you an invitation to come, and you tarry for weeks, it may seriously incommode them if you should pay them a visit of even a few days.

If no previous understanding has been had, the visit should be limited to three days, or a week at most.

While husbands and wives are always expected to accompany each other, where either may be invited, it is a trespass upon the generosity of the friend to take children and servants unless they are included in the invitation.

GENERAL RULES OF ETIQUETTE.

☞ Never send your guest, who is accustomed to a warm room, off into a cold, damp, spare bed to sleep.

☞ Never cross your legs and put out one foot in the street-car aisle or places where it will trouble others when passing by.

☞ Never examine the cards in the card-basket. While they may be exposed in the drawing-room, you are not expected to turn them over unless invited to do so.

☞ Never should a lady accept expensive gifts at the hands of a gentleman not related or engaged to her. However, gifts of flowers, books, music, or confectionery may be accepted.

You should not treat your friend's house as if it was a hotel, making your calls, visiting, transacting business about the town, and coming and going at all hours to suit your own convenience.

Having received intelligence of the expected arrival of a guest, have a carriage at the depot to meet the friend. Various members of the family being with the carriage will make the welcome more pleasant.

Take the baggage-checks, and give personal attention to having the trunks conveyed to your residence, relieving the guest of all care in the matter.

Have a warm, pleasant room especially prepared for the guest, with the dressing-table being supplied with water, soap, towel, comb, hair-brush, brush-broom, hat-brush, pomade, cologne, matches, needles, and pins.

The Etiquette of the Table.

he dinner hour will completely test the refinement, culture, and good breeding that the individual may possess. To appear advantageously at the table, the person must not only understand the laws of etiquette, but he must have the advantage of polite society. It is the province of this chapter to show what the laws of the table are. It will be the duty of the reader, in the varied relations of life, to make such use of them as circumstances shall permit.

ETIQUETTE FOR HOSTS AND HOSTESSES.

Having determined upon the number of guests to be invited, the next thing in order will be the issuing of notes of invitation by special messenger, which should be sent out ten or twelve days before the dinner is given.

For a very pleasant social affair the rule is not to have the company when seated exceed twelve in number. None of them should be conspicuously superior to the others, and all should be from the same circle of society.

The hour having arrived, the host offers his right arm to the most honored or possibly the eldest lady guest, and the gentleman most distinguished will escort the lady of the house.

Let us hope if there is any carving, it will be done before the meat is brought to the table, and the time of the company saved from this sometimes slow and tedious work.

It is customary for the gentleman who is the head of the household, in the ordinary family circle, to sit at the side of the table, in the center, having plates at his right hand, with food nearby. When all the family are seated, and all is in readiness, he will serve the guests who may be present. He will next serve the eldest lady of the household, and then the ladies and gentlemen as they come in order.

The hostess will sit opposite her husband, and preside over the tea, sauces, etc.

Behavior to be Avoided at the Table.

☞ Never open your mouth when chewing.

☞ Never make noises with the mouth or throat.

☞ Never leave the table with food in the mouth.

☞ Never tip back in your chair nor lounge upon the table.

☞ Never permit yourself to use gestures, nor illustrations made with a knife or fork on the tablecloth.

☞ Never hold bones in your fingers while you eat from them.

☞ Never encourage a dog or cat to play with you at the table.

☞ Never explain at the table why certain foods do not agree with you.

☞ Never pick your teeth or put your hand in your mouth while eating.

☞ Never wipe your fingers on the tablecloth, nor clean them in your mouth. Use the napkin.

The illustration at right depicts some behavior to be avoided at the table: (1) tipping back on the chair, (2) eating with mouth too full, (3) feeding a dog from the table, (4) holding the knife improperly, (5) engaging in argument at mealtime, (6) lounging upon the table, (7) bringing an upset child to the table, (8) licking the plate clean, (9) coming to the table improperly dressed, (10) picking the teeth with fingers, (11) scratching the head and frequently getting up from the table without reason.

ETIQUETTE FOR GUESTS.

It is of the utmost importance that all of the company be punctual, arriving from ten to fifteen minutes before the appointed time. To be ten minutes late, keeping the dinner waiting, is a serious offense which no one should be guilty of.

Sit upright, neither too close nor too far away from the table. Open and spread upon your lap or breast a napkin if one is provided—otherwise a handkerchief. Do not be in haste; compose yourself; put your mind into a pleasant condition, and resolve to eat slowly.

Keep the hands from the table until your time comes to be served. It is rude to take knife and fork in hand and commence drumming on the table while you are waiting. Eccentricity should be avoided as much as possible at the table.

Possibly grace will be said by someone present, and the most respectful attention and quietude should be observed until the exercise is passed.

It is the most appropriate time, while you wait to be served, for you to put into practice your knowledge of small talk and pleasant words with those whom you are sitting near.

Do not be impatient to be served. With social chitchat and eating, the meal-time should always be prolonged from thirty minutes to an hour.

If soup comes first, and you do not desire it, you will simply say, "No, I thank you," but make no comment; or you may take it and eat as little as you choose.

The soup should be eaten with a medium-sized spoon, so slowly and carefully that you will drop none upon your person or the tablecloth.

Making an effort to get the last drop, and all unusual noise when eating, should be avoided.

If furnished with potatoes in small dishes, you will put the skins back into the dish again; and thus where there are side dishes all refuse should be placed in them. Otherwise potato-skins will be placed upon the tablecloth, and bones upon the side of the plate. If possible, avoid putting waste matter upon the cloth.

The gentleman, when a dish is brought, having seen the lady he escorted provided for, will help himself and pass it on. He will pay no attention to the other lady near him, but will leave that to her escort. In all cases he will be careful and attentive to the wants of the lady in his charge, ascertaining her wishes and issuing her orders to the waiters.

No polite guest will ever fastidiously smell or examine any article of food before tasting it. Such conduct would be an insult to those who have invited him. Neither will the host or hostess apologize for the cooking.

Etiquette demands that each member of the company remain at least an hour after

Incorrect position for holding knife and fork.

Correct position for holding knife and fork.

the dinner is finished, it being impolite to hurry away immediately.

Never expectorate at the table; also avoid sneezing or coughing. It is better to arise quietly from the table if you have occasion to do either. A sneeze is prevented by placing the finger firmly on the upper lip.

Never spit out bones, cherry pits, grape skins, etc., upon your plate. Quietly press them from your mouth upon the fork, and lay them upon the side of your plate.

Never allow the conversation at the table to drift into anything but chitchat. The consideration of deep and abstruse principles will impair digestion.

BEHAVIOR TO BE AVOIDED AT THE TABLE.

☞ Never allow butter, soup, or other food to remain on your whiskers.

☞ Never wear gloves at the table, unless your hands for some special reason are unfit to be seen.

☞ Never, when serving others, overload the plate nor force upon them delicacies which they decline.

☞ Never make a display when removing hair, insects, or other disagreeable things from your food. Place them quietly under the edge of your plate.

The Etiquette of the Street.

 adies and gentlemen, when meeting on the sidewalk, should always pass to the right. Should the sidewalk be narrow or dangerous, gentlemen will see that ladies are protected from injury.

In the evening, or whenever safety may require, a gentleman should give a lady his arm. It is not customary in other cases to do so on the street, unless with an elderly lady, or the couple be husband and wife.

A gentleman may take two ladies upon his arms, but under no circumstances should the lady take the arms of two gentlemen.

A gentleman will assist a lady over from an omnibus or carriage, without waiting for the formality of an introduction. When the service is thus performed, he will raise his hat, bow, and pass on.

No gentleman will smoke when walking with, or standing in the presence of, a lady standing in the street. He should remove the cigar from her presence entirely, even though permission may be granted to continue the smoking.

A gentleman should not bow from a window to a lady on the street, though he may bow slightly from the street upon being recognized by a lady in a window. Such recognition should, however, generally be avoided, as gossip is likely to attach undue importance to it when seen by others.

No gentleman should stand on the street corners, steps of hotels, or other public places and make remarks about ladies passing by.

A lady should have the escort of a gentleman in the evening. Gossip and scandal are best avoided, however, if she has someone from her home call for her at an appointed hour.

Ladies should avoid walking rapidly upon the street, as it is ungraceful and unbecoming. Running across the street in front of carriages is dangerous, and shows want of dignity.

Staring at people, spitting, looking back after they pass, saluting people across the

street, calling out loudly, or laughing at people as they go by are all evidences of ill-breeding.

When crossing the pavement, the lady should raise her dress with the right hand, a little above the ankle. To raise the dress with both hands is vulgar, and can be excused only when the mud is very deep.

Allowing a dress to trail on the street is in exceedingly bad taste. Such a street costume simply calls forth criticism and contempt from the more sensible people.

A true lady will go quietly and unobtrusively about her business when on the street, never seeking to attract the attention of the opposite sex, at the same time recognizing acquaintances with a courteous bow, and friends with pleasant words of greeting.

Swinging the arms when walking, eating upon the street, sucking the parasol handles, pushing violently through a crowd, talking and laughing very loudly and boisterously on the streets, and whispering in public conveyances are all evidences of ill-breeding in ladies.

General Rule of Etiquette.

☛ Never attempt to convey the impression that you are a genius by imitating the faults of distinguished men. Because certain great men were poor penmen, wore long hair, or had other peculiarities, it does not follow that you will be great by imitating their eccentricities.

THE ETIQUETTE OF THE PARTY AND THE BALL.

The entertainment you intend giving is larger than a dinner party. To it you will invite a greater number of your friends and associates, so great a number, indeed, of young and middle-aged people, that the serious question is, how will they be entertained? You conclude that you will allow them to dance, and you will name your entertainment a ball.

Each dancer should be provided with a ball-card bearing a printed programme of the dances, having a space for making engagements upon the same, with a small pencil attached.

Etiquette requires that the lady dance first with her escort, and afterward he should see that she is provided with partners, and that she enjoys herself, though she may dance with whom she pleases. He

THE EVILS OF THE BALL.

For the company to assemble at a late hour and engage in unusual, exciting, and severe exercise throughout the entire night is often too great a tax upon the physical system. To dress too thinly, and in a state of perspiration to be exposed, as ladies at the ball frequently are, to drafts of cold, is often times to plant the seeds of a disease from which they never recover.

Again, to come in contact, as ladies are liable to do, more especially at the public ball, with disreputable men, is sometimes to form alliances that will cause a lifetime of sorrow.

Well may the watchful parent look with anxiety and suspicion upon the ball, because its associations are so frequently dangerous. If in this chapter we may give admonitions and suggestions that shall tend to correct some of the evils of the dance, our labors will not be in vain.

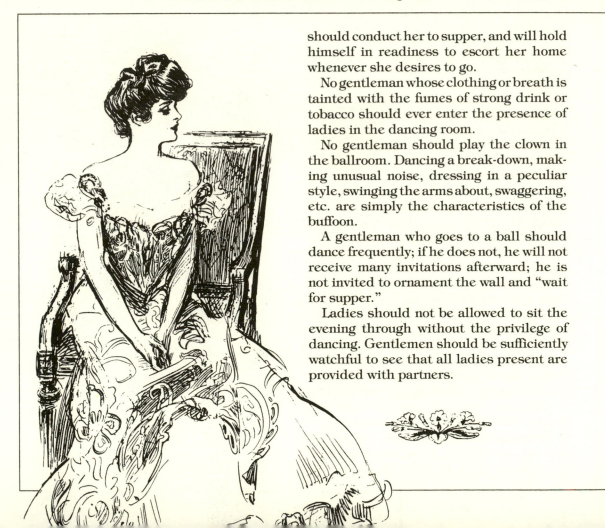

should conduct her to supper, and will hold himself in readiness to escort her home whenever she desires to go.

No gentleman whose clothing or breath is tainted with the fumes of strong drink or tobacco should ever enter the presence of ladies in the dancing room.

No gentleman should play the clown in the ballroom. Dancing a break-down, making unusual noise, dressing in a peculiar style, swinging the arms about, swaggering, etc. are simply the characteristics of the buffoon.

A gentleman who goes to a ball should dance frequently; if he does not, he will not receive many invitations afterward; he is not invited to ornament the wall and "wait for supper."

Ladies should not be allowed to sit the evening through without the privilege of dancing. Gentlemen should be sufficiently watchful to see that all ladies present are provided with partners.

The orchestra will first play a march, then a quadrille, a waltz, a polka, a gallop, etc. interspersed with several round dances to each quadrille, usually ending with a march prior to supper.

Never eat your supper in gloves. White kid gloves should be worn at other times throughout the dancing. It is well to have two pairs, one before supper, and one afterward.

If any lady is without an attendant, it should be the duty of the lady of the house to see that she is provided with an escort. After supper, several dances will follow, the company dispersing, let us hope, at an early, temperate hour.

The lady is not obliged to invite her escort to enter the house when he accompanies her home, and if invited he should decline the invitation. He should request permission to call the next day or evening, which will be true politeness.

A gentleman should never presume upon the acquaintance of a lady after a ball. Ballroom introductions close with the dancing. Ladies will consult their own pleasure about recognizing a ballroom acquaintance at a future meeting.

Behavior to be Avoided at the Ball.

☛ A lady should not enter or cross the hall unattended.

☛ No gentleman should ever enter the ladies' dressing room at a ball.

☛ Never lead a lady in the ball by the hand; always offer the arm.

☛ A lady should not select a gentleman to hold her bouquet, fan, and gloves during the dance, unless he be her husband, escort, or a relative.

☛ Do not engage yourself for the last two or three dances; it may keep you too late.

☛ Neither married nor unmarried ladies should leave a ballroom unattended.

☛ A gentleman in waltzing should not encircle the waist of a lady until the dancing commences, and he should drop his arm when the music ceases.

☛ No gentleman should use his bare hand to press the waist of a lady in the waltz. If without gloves, he should carry a handkerchief in his hand.

How to Entertain at the Party.

Should any lady-guest be invited to play the piano, it is courtesy for the gentleman nearest to her to offer his arm and escort her to the instrument. While she is playing he will hold her bouquet, fan, and gloves. He should also turn the leaves if he can readily read music, but he should not attempt it otherwise. It is very impolite to speak disparagingly of the piano, however much it may be out of tune.

Among the methods of entertainment resorted to, aside from conversation and dancing, may be those of a literary character. Thus, a debatable question may be propounded, a presiding officer selected, assisted by two, four, or six others, two leading disputants appointed, debaters chosen upon each side, and the speakers given each two, three, or five minutes to talk; the president and board of arbitration

to decide the question according to the weight of the argument.

Croquet parties are very fashionable, and are a healthful, pleasant means of diversion. The essentials necessary to make the game pleasant are good grounds that can be shaded, and clean, comfortable, cool seats.

It is the duty of the gentlemen to be ever attentive to the ladies. If it be a picnic, the gentlemen will carry the luncheon, erect the swings, construct the tables, bring the water, and provide the fuel for boiling the tea.

On fishing excursions, they will furnish the tackle, bait the hooks, row the boats, carry the fish, and furnish comfortable seats for the ladies. In gathering nuts, they will climb the trees, do the shaking, carry the nuts, and assist the ladies across the streets and over the fences.

THE ETIQUETTE OF TRAVELLING.

The reader will call to mind people who always appear at ease when they are traveling. Investigation will prove that these individuals have usually had a wide experience in journeying, and an extensive acquaintance with the world. The experienced traveler has learned the necessity of always being on time, of having baggage checked early, of purchasing a ticket before entering the cars, and of procuring a seat in a good location before the car is full.

The inexperienced traveler is readily known by his flurry and mistakes. He is likely to be behind time, and he is likely to be an hour too early. For want of explicit direction, his baggage often fails to reach the train in time, or does not come at all. His trunks, from lack of strength, are liable

to be easily broken. In his general confusion, when he buys a ticket he neglects to place it where it will be secure, and consequently loses it. He forgets a portion of his baggage, and thus in a dozen ways he is likely to be in trouble.

People with weak eyes should avoid reading on the train, and those having weak lungs should avoid much talking, as an undue effort will be required to talk above the noise of the train.

Passengers should avoid eating at irregular times on the journey, and gentlemen should avoid smoking in the presence of those to whom it may be offensive.

Avoid wearing laces, velvets, or any articles that naturally accumulate and hold dust. Excessive finery or a lavish display of jewelry are in bad taste on extended journeys.

A lady and gentleman should avoid evidences of undue familiarity in the presence of strangers. Couples who may evince a silly affection by overfondling of each other in public make themselves appear extremely ridiculous to all who may see them.

Ladies and gentlemen who are strangers, being thrown into the company of each other for a long journey, need not necessarily refuse to speak to each other. While the lady should be guarded, acquaintance may be made with certain reserve.

If the gentleman is an authorized escort, he should purchase the needed confections and literature on the train. He should be fruitful in the introduction of topics that will enliven, amuse, and instruct the lady, if she is inclined to be reticent.

ETIQUETTE FOR THE UNATTENDED LADY AT THE HOTEL.

The unattended lady should enter a hotel by the ladies' entrance. When in the parlor, she should send for the proprietor or clerk, present her card, and state the length of time that she designs to remain.

By request, the waiter will meet the lady at the entrance to the dining room and conduct her to a seat, thus saving her the necessity of crossing the room without an escort.

Professor Hill's Guide to Love and Marriage

et no lady commence and continue a correspondence with a view to marriage, for fear that she may never have another opportunity. It is the mark of judgment and rare good sense to go through life without wedlock, if she cannot marry from love. Somewhere in eternity, the poet tells us, our true mate will be found.

Do not be afraid of being an "old maid." The disgrace attached to that term has long since passed away.

Unmarried ladies of mature years are proverbially among the most intelligent, accomplished, and independent to be found in society.

The sphere of a woman's action and work is so widening that she can today, if she desires, handsomely and independently support herself. She need not, therefore, marry for a home.

Above all, no lady should allow herself to correspond with an intemperate man with a view to matrimony. She may reform him, but the chances are that her life's happi-

ness will be completely destroyed by such a union. Better, a thousand times, the single, free, and independent maidenhood, than for a woman to trail her life in the dust, and bring poverty, shame, and disgrace on her children, by marrying a man addicted to dissipated habits.

Let no man make it an ultimate object in life to marry a rich wife. It is not the posses-sion, but the acquisition, of wealth, that gives happiness.

It is a generally conceded fact that the inheritance of great wealth is a positive mental and moral injury to young men, completely destroying the stimulus to advancement.

Let no couple hesitate to marry because they are poor. It will cost them less to live

after marriage than before—one light, one fire, etc., answering the purpose for both. Having an object to live for, also, they will commence their accumulations after marriage as never before.

The young woman that demands a certain amount of costly style, beyond the income of her betrothed, no young man should ever wed. As a general thing, however, women have common sense, and, if husbands will perfectly confide in their wives, telling them exactly their pecuniary condition, the wife will live within the husband's income. In the majority of cases where men fail in business, the failure being attributed to the wife's extravagance, the wife has been kept in entire ignorance of her husband's pecuniary resources.

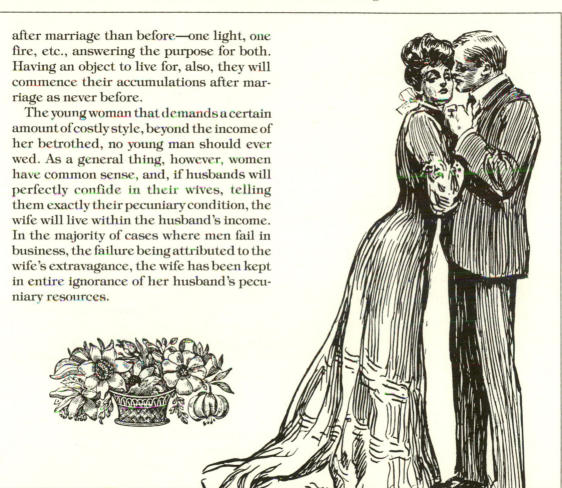

Love Letters.

The love letter is the prelude to marriage—a state that, if the husband and wife be fitted for each other, is the most natural, and serenely happy; a state, however, that none should enter upon, until, in judgement and physical development, both parties have completely matured. Many a life has been wrecked by a blind, impulsive marriage, simply resulting from a youthful passion. As a physiological law, man should be 25, and woman 23, before marrying.

Of all letters, the love letter should be the most carefully prepared. Among the written missives, they are the most thoroughly read and re-read, the longest preserved, and the most likely to be regretted in the afterlife.

They should be written with the utmost regard for perfection. An ungrammatical expression, or word improperly spelled, may seriously interfere with the writer's

prospects, by being turned to ridicule.

As a rule, the love letter should be very guardedly written. Ladies, especially, should be very careful to maintain their dignity when writing them, when, possibly, after time the feelings entirely change, you will regret that you wrote the letter at all. If the love remains unclaimed, no harm will certainly be done if you wrote with judgement and care.

While there may be exceptional cases, as a rule, correspondence should be conducted only with the assent and approval of the parents. If it is not so, parents are themselves generally to blame.

No woman, who is a lady, will be guilty of making light of the sentiments that are expressed to her in a letter.

No man, who is a gentleman, will boast of his love conquests, among companions, or reveal to others the correspondence between himself and a lady.

If an engagement is mutually broken off, all the love letters should be returned. To retain them is dishonorable. They were written under circumstances that no longer exist. It is better for both parties to wash out every recollection of the past, by returning to the giver every memento of the dead love.

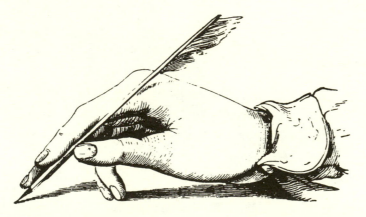

HOW TO BEGIN A LOVE CORRESPONDENCE.

Some gentlemen, being very favorably impressed with a lady at first sight, and having no immediate opportunity for introduction, make bold, after learning her name, to write her at once, seeking an interview, the form of which letter will be found hereafter. A gentleman in doing so, however, runs considerable risk of receiving a rebuff from the lady, though not always.

Miss Myra Bronson:

Having greatly enjoyed our brief meeting at the residence of Mrs. Powell last Thursday evening, I venture to write to request permission to call on you at your own residence. Though myself almost entirely a stranger in the city, your father told me the other evening that he remembers Mr. Williams of Syracuse, who is my uncle. Trusting that you will pardon this liberty, and place me on your list of gentleman acquaintances, I am,

    Yours, Very Respectfully,
    Harmon Williams.

Favorable Reply:

Mr. Harmon Williams
    Dear Sir:
    It will give me much pleasure to see you at our residence next Wednesday evening. My father desires me to state that he retains a very favorable recollection of your uncle, in consequence of which he will be pleased to continue your acquaintance.
    Yours Truly,
    Myra Bronson.

Unfavorable Reply:

Miss Myra Bronson, making it a rule to receive no gentleman visitors upon such brief acquaintance, begs to decline the honor of Mr. Williams' visits.

To a Lady, from a Gentleman Confessing Change of Sentiment:

Miss Marion Thornton:

Your note accusing me of coldness is before me. After spending several hours in a consideration of this subject, to determine what is my duty, I have concluded that it is decidedly best for me to be perfectly frank with you, and give my reasons for a change of sentiment.

I do not think we could live happily together if we were married because, from disparaging remarks I have heard you make concerning people that are not wealthy, I think you would be entirely dissatisfied with my circumstances.

The further fact that you allow your mother to do all the drudgery of the household, you sitting in the parlor entertaining gentlemen, and affecting to have no knowledge of housekeeping, is proof that our tastes would not accord in home matters.

I consider it just as honorable, and just as important, that young ladies should do something to support themselves, as that young men should. If the opportunities are not as great for them to go abroad, they can, at least while at home, learn to be good in sewing, cooking, and housekeep-

ing, and thus be prepared when opportunities offer, to make prudent, economical, tidy housewives.

I do not under-value the importance of being proficient in the lighter accomplishments which go to make a lady at ease in society; but I vastly more prize the lady who knows how to get an excellent breakfast early in the morning, who is not only a model of neatness herself, but relieves her mother in household duties, keeping her younger brothers and sisters clean and orderly.

I have admired and loved you for your musical talent and your fine conversational powers, but, as I could not keep the necessary servants to enable you constantly to gratify those talents to the exclusion of the more substantial duties, I feel that our marriage would be a mistake for us both.

You asked my reason for my changing love; I have reluctantly, yet plainly, stated it. Hoping, however, that you may always be happy in life, I am,

Your Friend,
Clinton Holmes.

A Good Way of Breaking the Ice:

My Dear Friend Caroline:

I returned yesterday from a brief trip into Canada, my journey being most agreeable; only one little episode breaking the monotony, as I neared home, which was this: In the next seat behind me in the car sat a young couple, who were evidently regretting that their ride was so near an end.

Though buried in my reading, I could not avoid hearing much that they said. One question asked by the young man made a striking impression on my mind. "Maggie," said he, "we have now been acquainted a good while; you know me, and I know you. I do not need to tell you that I love you with all my heart; now, do you love me?"

I knew the young fellow had taken that occasion, when the cars were thundering along, so that he might not be knocked down by the beating of his own heart.

I confess to have been guilty of eavesdropping. Then I listened intently for the lady's answer, but just at that moment, as my ill luck would have it, another train came thundering by us, and her voice was drowned in the noise. I got to thinking like this: suppose you and I were riding thus, and I should ask precisely the same question; what would be your reply? I am very curious to know what your answer would be, and shall await a letter from you with much anxiety.

Most Truly Yours,
Roland Mills.

Reply to a Young Man that Uses Tobacco:

Mr. Bannister:

Dear Sir:

I am in receipt of your courteous letter, containing a declaration of love. I will be frank enough with you to admit that, while I have been sensible of your affectionate regard for me for some months, I have also cherished a growing interest in you. In truth, to make a candid confession, I most sincerely love you. I should, perhaps, say no more, but I feel it due to you, as well as to myself, to be strictly honest in my expression, lest we foster this growing love, which, under present conditions, must be broken off.

I have always admired your natural ability; I appreciate you for your industry; I respect you for your filial conduct toward your parents. In fact, I consider you quite a model young man, were it not for one habit, which has always been, heretofore, a very delicate subject for me to speak of, fearing that it might give you offense. But believing it best that I be true to my convictions and state my objections plainly, I thus freely write them.

I have reference to the use of tobacco.

Apparently, this is a little thing. I am aware that ladies generally consider it beneath their notice; but so thoroughly convinced am I that it is one of the most destructive habits, sapping the morality and vigor of our young men, that I could never consent to wed a man addicted to its use, my reasons being as follows:

It would impoverish my home. Only 10 cents a day expended for a cigar, in a lifetime of 40 years, with its accumulations of interest, amounts to over $4000! The little sum of 11 cents per day, saved from being squandered on tobacco, and properly put at interest, amounts in that time to over $5000! No wonder so many homes, the heads of which use tobacco, are without the comforts of life.

It might wreck my happiness. It is a well-known physiological fact that the use of tobacco deadens the sense of taste; that water and all common drinks become insipid and tasteless when tobacco is used, so that the person using the same involuntarily craves strong drink, in order to taste it.

Therein lies the foundation of a large share of the drunkenness of the country.

Observation proves that, while many men use tobacco that are not drunkards, almost every drunkard is a user of tobacco, having nearly always formed the habit from the use of this narcotic weed.

It would surround me with filth. To say nothing of the great drain on the physical health by the constant expectoration of saliva, thus ruining the health of many robust constitutions, I could not endure the fetid breath of the tobacco-user.

I sicken at the thought of the brown saliva exuding from between the lips; physiology proving that, with tobacco-chewers, nearly all the waste fluids from the body pass through the mouth.

I am immediately faint at the thought of dragging my skirts through spittle in a railway car, or any place where it is thrown upon the floor; I turn with disgust at the atmosphere—God's pure, fresh air—that is tainted with the stench of tobacco smoke.

It would corrupt my husband's morality.

All the associations of tobacco are bad. It is true that many good men use tobacco. It is also a truth that nearly every man that is bad is addicted to its use. To smoke in peace, the man must resort to the place where others smoke. In that room are profanity, obscene language, and every species of vulgarity. There may be occasionally an exception. The fact is patent, however, that, in the room in which vulgarity and obscenity prevail, there is always smoke in the air, and spittle on the floor.

You will forgive me for speaking thus plainly. I love you too well to disguise my feelings on the subject. I could not possibly constantly love a tobacco-user, for the reasons that I have given.

While I devotedly love you, I cannot consent that you should bestow your affections upon a person that would instinctively repel you. Believing, therefore, under the circumstances, that our further correspondence should cease, I remain,

Your Friend and Well-Wisher,
Marietta Wilcox.

A Gentleman Makes a Frank Acknowledgment, Gushing with Sentiment, and Running Over with Poetry:

My Dear Mary:

One by one the brown leaves are falling, reminding us that the golden summer that we have so delightfully loitered through approaches its close. How thickly our pathway has been strewn with roses; how fragrant have been the million blossoms; how sweetly the birds have sung; how beautiful have been the sunny days; how joyous have been the starry nights!

Dear Mary, I do not need to tell you that this delightful summer has been to me one grand Elysian scene. I have gazed on and dreamed of thy beauty. I have been fed by thy sparkling repartee and merriment; I have drunk at the fountain of thy intellect, but the feast is ended, and gradually the curtain is falling.

Dear, beautiful summer; so beautiful to me because of thy loved presence. And standing, now on the threshold of a scene all changed, I take a last, fond look on the beautiful picture that will return to me no more; and yet, who knows, but on in that great eternity we may live again these Eden hours.

Dearest, you must forgive my ardent expressions in this letter. With a temperament gushing to the brim and overflowing with sentiment and rhapsody, I have passed the fleeting summer in thy charming presence in one continual dream of poetry.

I cannot now turn back to the solemn duties before me without telling you what trembled on my tongue a thousand times, as we gathered flowers together and wove our chaplets in the sunny days gone by.

Dear, darling Mary, I love you, I adore you. How often in the beautiful moonlit nights, as we strolled among the lilacs and the primroses, have I been on the verge of clasping your jeweled hand and telling you all my heart. But, oh! I did not quite dare; the hours were so delightful, even as they were.

Fearing that I might be repulsed, I chose to accept the joy even that there was, rather than run the risk of losing it all.

How many a morning have I arisen and firmly resolved that, ere another day, I would know my fate. But, ah! the twilight would fall, and the evening hour would pass by, and I never completely dared to risk the result of a declaration. The morrow I knew would be joyous if I bridled my impulse. It might not be if I made a mistake. But the dream has passed by.

Tomorrow, I bid adieu to these sylvan groves, the quiet meadows, and the gurgling brooks, to go back to the prose duties of business. And now, at the close of this festal season, as I am upon the verge of going, having nothing to lose and everything to gain, I have told you my heart. I have not the slightest idea what your reply will be. You have been to me one continual puzzle. If your answer is adverse, I can only entertain the highest respect for you ever in the future, and memory shall keep alive the recollection of the most blissful summer I have ever known.

If your reply is favorable—dearest, may I fondly hope that it will be?—then opens before me a great volume of happiness, of which this joyous summer has been but the opening chapter.

Dear Mary, may I come again and see you, and address you henceforth as a lover? The messenger who brings you this will return again in an hour for your answer. I need not tell you what an hour of suspense this will be to me. Upon your reply hangs my future.

If your reply is favorable, I shall tarry not another day; and will you grant me a long interview, as I have much to talk over with you? If unfavorable, please return this letter with your note. Accept my warmest thanks for the entertainment which I, in common with others, have received at your hand in the past; and, if I may not sign myself your devoted lover, I shall at least, I trust, have ever the pleasure of subscribing myself,

Your Sincere Friend,
Clarence Harrington.

Favorable Reply:

Dear Clarence:

I shall not attempt in this to answer your missive with the same poetic fervor that colors your letter from beginning to end. While it is given you to tread the emerald pavements of an imaginative Eden, in my plainer nature I can only walk the common earth.

I fully agree with you in your opinion of the beautiful summer just passed. Though in seasons heretofore many people have been here from the cities, I have never known a summer so delightful. Yes, Clarence, these three months have been joyous, because—shall I confess it?—because you have been here. I need not write more. I shall be at home this afternoon, at two o'clock, and will be happy to see you.

Yours Very Truly,
Mary Singleton.

PERSONAL ADVERTISEMENTS.

PERSONAL: Will the lady who rode up Broadway last Thursday afternoon, about two o'clock, in an omnibus getting out at Stewart's, accompanied by a little girl dressed in a blue suit, please send her address to D.B.M., Herald Office?

It is useless to advise people never to reply to a personal advertisement like the above. To do so is like totally refusing young people the privilege of dancing. People will dance, and they will answer personal advertisements.

The best course, therefore, is to properly direct the dancers and caution the writers in their answers to newspaper personals. If the eye of the young lady referred to meets

the above advertisement, she will possibly be indignant at first, and will, perhaps, resolve to pay no attention to it.

It will continue to occupy her attention so much, however, and curiosity will become so great, that, in order to ease her mind, she will at last give her address, in which case she makes a very serious mistake, as any lady replying to a communication of such a character, giving her name and residence to a stranger, places herself at a great disadvantage.

Should her communication never be answered, she will feel mortified ever afterwards that she committed the indiscretion of replying to the advertisement at all; and, should the person she addresses prove to be some worthless fellow who may presume to press an acquaintance upon the strength of her reply, it may cause her very serious perplexity and embarrassment.

It is clearly evident, therefore, that she should not give her name and address as requested; and yet, as the advertisement may refer to a business matter of importance, or bring about an acquaintance that she will not regret, she may relieve her curiosity on the subject by writing the following note in reply:

The Reply:

D.B.M.: I found the above advertisement in the Herald of this morning. I suppose myself to be the person referred to. You will please state your object in addressing me, with references.

Address, A.L.K., Herald Office.

It is probable that the advertiser, if a gentleman, will reply, giving his reasons for requesting the lady's address, with references, upon receiving, which the lady will do as she may choose relative to continuing the correspondence. In either case, it will be seen that she has in no way compromised her dignity, and she retains the advantage of knowing the motive and object that prompted the advertisement, while she is yet unknown to the advertiser.

Great caution should be exercised in answering personals. The supposition is, if the advertiser be a gentleman, that he will honorably seek an interview with a lady, and pay court as gentlemen ordinarily do. Still, an occasion may happen to a man, who is in the highest sense a gentleman, wherein he sees the lady that he very greatly admires, and can learn her address in no other way without rendering himself offensive and impertinent; hence, the apparent necessity of the above personal advertisement.

Instances have also occurred where gentlemen, driven with business, and having but little time to mingle in female society, or no opportunity, being strangers comparatively, desirous of forming the acquain-

tance of ladies, have honestly advertised for correspondence, been honestly answered, and marriage was the result.

Those advertisements, however, wherein Sammy Brown and Coney Smith advertise for correspondence with any number of young ladies, for *"fun, mutual improvement, and what may grow out of it, photographs exchanged, etc.,"* young ladies should be very wary of answering.

Instances have been known where scores of young ladies, having answered such an advertisement, could they have looked in upon those young men, a week afterwards, would have seen them with a pile of photo-graphs and letters, exhibiting them to their companions, and making fun of the girls who had been so foolish as to answer their advertisement.

It is true that no one but the meanest kind of a rascal would be guilty of such a disgraceful act as to advertise for and expose correspondence thus, and it is equally true that the young lady who gives the advertiser the opportunity to ridicule her shows herself to be very foolish.

Natural Selection.

n the first place, observation proves that selections made in nature by the beasts of the field and fowls of the air, of couples which pair, the male is always the strongest, generally the largest, the most brave and always the leader.

The female follows, trusting to her companion, leaving him to fight the heavy battles, apparently confident in his bravery, strength, and wisdom.

If nature teaches anything, it is what observation and experience in civilized life has also proved correct, that of husband and wife, rightly mated, the husband should represent the positive—the physical forces, the intellectual and the strongly loving; while the wife will represent the negative—the sympathetic, the spiritual, and the affectionate.

The husband should be so strong as to be a natural protector to his family. He should be brave, that he may defend his companion. He should be wise, and he should be so thoroughly true and devoted to his wife that he will delight in being her guardian and support.

The wife, confident in her husband's strength and wisdom, will thus implicitly yield to his protecting care. And thus both will be happy in exercising the prerogatives which belong naturally to the guardian and protector; and she in her confidence, love and respect for her companion whom she can implicitly trust.

WHOM TO MARRY.

☞ Marry a person whom you have known long enough to be sure of his or her worth—if not personally, at least by reputation.

☞ Marry a person who is your equal in societal position. If there be a difference either way, let the husband be superior to the wife. It is difficult for a wife to love and honor a person whom she is compelled to look down upon.

Peculiarities Suitable for Each Other.

Those who are neither very tall nor very short, whose eyes are neither very black nor very blue, whose hair is neither very black nor very red—the mixed types—may marry those who are quite similar in form, complexion, and temperament to themselves.

Bright red hair and a florid complexion indicate an excitable temperament. Such should marry the jet-black hair and the brunette type.

The gray, blue, black, or hazel eyes should not marry those of the same color. Where the color is very pronounced, the union should be with those of a decidedly different color.

The very corpulent should unite with the thin and spare and the short, thick-set should choose a different constitution.

The thin, bony, wiry, prominent-featured, Roman-nosed, cold-blooded individual should marry the round-featured, warm-hearted, and emotional. Thus, the cool should unite with warmth and susceptibility.

The extremely irritable and nervous should unite with the sympathetic, the slow, and the quiet. Thus, the stolid will be prompted by the nervous companion, while the excitable will be quieted by the gentleness of the less nervous.

The quick-motioned, rapid-speaking person should marry the calm and deliberate. The warmly impulsive should unite with the stoical.

The very fine-haired, soft, and delicate-skinned should not marry those like themselves; and the curly should unite with the straight and smooth hair.

The thin, long-face should marry the round-favored; and the flat nose should marry the full Roman. The woman who inherits the features and peculiarities of her father should marry a man who partakes of the characteristics of his mother; but in all these cases where the type is not pronounced, but is, on the contrary, an average or medium, those forms, features, and temperaments may marry either.

ETIQUETTE OF COURTSHIP.

adies should not allow courtship to be conducted at unseasonable hours. The evening entertainment, the walk, the ride, are all favorable for the study of each other's tastes and feelings. For the gentleman to protract his visit at the lady's residence until a late hour is almost sure to give offense to the lady's parents, and is extremely ungentlemanly.

However suitable may be the physical characteristics, there are many other matters to be considered before a man and woman may take upon themselves the obligation to love and serve each other through life, and these can only be learned by acquaintance and courtship, concerning which the following suggestions may be appropriate:

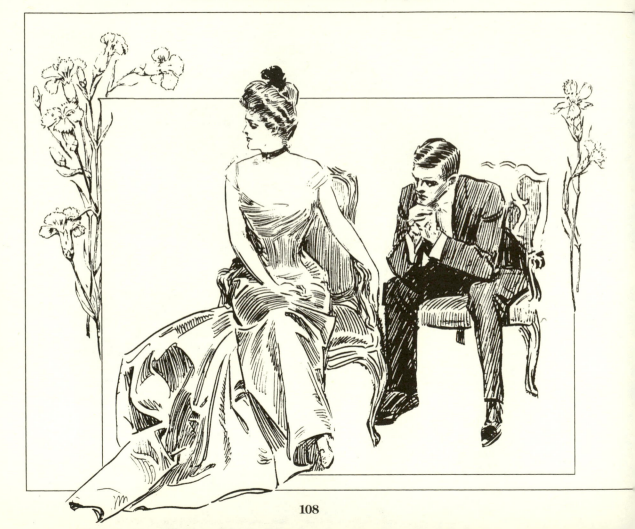

Any gentleman who may continuously give special, undivided attention to a certain lady, is presumed to do so because he prefers her to others. It is reasonable to suppose that others will observe his action. It is also to be expected that the lady will herself appreciate the fact, and her feelings are likely to become engaged.

Should she allow an intimacy thus to ripen upon the part of the gentleman, and to continue, it is to be expected that he will be encouraged to hope for her hand; and hence it is the duty of both lady and gentleman, if neither intends marriage, to discourage an undue intimacy which may ripen into love, as it is in the highest degree dishonorable to trifle with the affections of another. If, however, neither has objections to the other, the courtship may continue.

THE DECISIVE QUESTION.

t length the time arrives for the gentleman to make a proposal. If he is a good judge of human nature, he will have discovered long ere this whether his favors have been acceptably received or not, and yet he may not know positively how the lady will receive an offer of marriage. It becomes him, therefore, to propose.

What shall he say? There are many ways whereby he may introduce the subject. Among these are the following:

☛ He may write to the lady, making an offer, and request her to reply. He may, if he dare not trust to words, even in her presence write the question on a slip of paper, and request her laughingly to give a plain "no" or "yes."

☞ He may ask her if a gentleman very much like himself were to make a proposal of marriage to her, what she would say. She will probably laughingly reply that it will be time enough to tell what she would say when the proposal is made. And so the ice would be broken.

☞ He may jokingly remark that he intends one of these days to ask a certain lady not a thousand miles away if she will marry him, and asks her what answer she supposes the lady will give him; she will quite likely reply that it will depend upon what lady he asks. And thus he may approach the subject, by agreeable and easy stages, in a hundred ways, depending upon the circumstances.

THE WEDDING.

he wedding-day having arrived, the presents for the bride, if there be any, which may be sent at any time during the previous week, will be handsomely displayed before the ceremony. The presents, which have the names of the donors attached, are for the bride, never the bridegroom, although many of them may be sent by friends of the latter.

Only the bridegroom is congratulated at the wedding; it is he who is supposed to have won the prize. Acquaintances of both should speak to the bride first; but if acquainted with but one, they will address that one first, when introductions will take place.

In arranging the preliminaries, the bride may act her pleasure in regard to bridesmaids. She may have none; she may have one, two, three, four, six, or eight. While in England it is customary to have but one groomsman, it is not uncommon in the

United States to have one groomsman for every bridesmaid.

The bridegroom should make the first groomsman the manager of affairs, and should furnish him with money to pay necessary expenses.

The bridegroom should send a carriage at his expense for the officiating clergyman and his family. He is not expected to pay for the carriage of the parents of the bride, nor for those occupied by the bridesmaids and groomsmen.

The latter will furnish the carriages for the ladies, unless otherwise provided. The invited guests will go in carriages at their own expense.

The bride goes to the church in a carriage, accompanied by her parents, or those who stand to her in the relation of parents (as may other relatives, or legal guardian), or she may be accompanied by the bridesmaids.

When a ring is used, it is the duty of the first bridesmaid to remove the bride's left-hand glove. An awkward pause is, however, avoided by opening one seam of the glove upon the ring finger, and at the proper time the glove may be turned back, and the ring thus easily placed where it belongs, which is the third finger of the left hand.

The responses of the bride and groom should not be too hastily nor too loudly given.

Following the ceremony, the parents of the bride speak to her first, succeeded by the parents of the groom before other friends.

The bride and groom, after the ceremony, will go in the same carriage from the church to the home or to the depot.

THE WIFE'S DUTY IN MARRIAGE.

Never should a wife display her best conduct, her accomplishments, her smiles, and her best nature, exclusively away from home.

Be careful in your purchases. Let your husband know what you buy, and that you have wisely expended your money.

Let no wife devote a large portion of her time to society-work which shall keep her away from home daytime and evenings, without the full concurrence of her husband.

Beware of entrusting the confidence of your household to outside parties. The moment you discuss the faults of your husband with another, that moment an element of discord has been admitted which will one day rend your family circle.

If in moderate circumstances, do not be over ambitious to make an expensive display in your rooms. With your own work you can embellish at a cheap price, and yet very handsomely, if you have taste. Let the adornings of your private rooms be largely the work of your own hands.

Beware of bickering about little things. Your husband returns from his labors with his mind absorbed in business. In his dealings with his employees, he is in the habit of giving commands and of being obeyed.

In his absent-mindedness, he does not realize, possibly, the change from his business to his home, and the same dictatorial spirit may possess him in the domestic circle. Should such be the case, avoid all disputes.

What matters it where a picture hangs, or a flower vase may sit? Make the home so charming and so wisely ordered that your husband will gladly be relieved of its care, and will willingly yield up its entire management to yourself.

Be always very careful of your conduct and language. A husband is largely restrained by the chastity, purity, and refinement of his wife.

A lowering of dignity, a looseness of expression, and vulgarity of words, may greatly lower the standard of the husband's purity of speech and morals.

Whatever may have been the cares of the day, greet your husband with a smile when he returns. Make your personal appearance just as beautiful as possible. Your dress may be made of calico, but it should be neat. Let him enter rooms so attractive and sunny that all the recollections of his home, when away from the same, shall attract him back.

Be careful that you do not estimate your husband solely by his ability to make display. The nature of his employment, in comparison with others, may not be favorable for fine show, but that should matter not. The superior qualities of mind and heart alone will bring permanent happiness.

To have a cheerful, pleasant home awaiting the husband is not all. He may bring a guest whom he desires to favorably impress, and upon you will devolve the duty of entertaining the visitor so agreeably that the husband shall take pride in you.

THE HUSBAND'S DUTY.

Every grave responsibility has the man assumed in his marriage. Doting parents have confided to his care the welfare of a loved daughter, and a trusting woman has risked all her future happiness in his keeping. Largely, it will depend upon him whether her pathway shall be strewn with thorns or roses.

Let your wife understand fully your business. In nearly every case she will be found a most valuable adviser when she understands all your circumstances.

Do not be dictatorial in the family circle. The home is the wife's province. It is her natural field of labor. It is her right to govern and direct its interior management. You would not expect her to come to your shop, your office, your store, or your farm, to give orders on how your work should be conducted. Neither should you interfere with the duties that legitimately belong to her.

If a dispute arises, dismiss the subject with a kind word, and do not seek to carry your point by discussion. It is a glorious achievement to master one's own temper. You may discover that you are in error, and if your wife is wrong, she will gladly, in her cooler moments, acknowledge the fault.

Having confided to the wife all your business affairs, determine with her what your income will be in the coming year. Afterwards ascertain what your household expenses will necessarily be, and then set aside a weekly sum, which should regularly and invariably be paid the wife at a stated time.

Let this sum be even more than enough, so that the wife can pay all bills, and have the satisfaction besides of accumulating a fund of her own, with which she can exercise a spirit of independence in the bestowal of charity, the purchase of a gift, or any article she may desire. You may be sure that the wife will very seldom use the money unwisely, if the husband gives her his entire confidence.

Your wife, possibly, is inexperienced; perhaps she is delicate in health, also, and matters that would be of little concern to you may weigh heavily upon her. She needs, therefore, your tenderest approval, your sympathy, and gentle advice.

When her efforts are crowned with success, be sure that you give her praise. Few husbands realize how happy the wife is made by the knowledge that her efforts and her merits are appreciated. There are times, also, when the wife's variable condition of health will be likely to make her cross and petulant. The husband must overlook all this, even if the wife is at times unreasonable.

INDEX